RON DESANTIS BOOK

The Biography of Ron DeSantis

by

Real Facts

Important Legal Information

Disclaimer

This book's contents are solely for educational and informative purposes. We take no responsibility for any impacts or outcomes that may occur as a result of using this content. Despite making every attempt to offer accurate and sufficient information, the author accepts no responsibility for its correctness, usage, or abuse.

Table of Contents

Introduction

Welcome to the captivating biography of Ron DeSantis, an American politician and former military officer serving as the 46th governor of Florida. In this book, we delve deep into the life and accomplishments of a man who has made a significant impact on the political landscape of Florida and the nation. From his humble beginnings to his rise to power, we explore the untold story of Ron DeSantis and shed light on the experiences and decisions that have shaped his remarkable journey.

Ron DeSantis was born on September 14, 1978, in Jacksonville, Florida. Raised in a middle-class family, he learned the values of hard work, perseverance, and patriotism from an early age. As a child, DeSantis exhibited a natural curiosity and a keen interest in public service. These early qualities would later lay the foundation for his remarkable career.

This biography aims to provide readers with a comprehensive understanding of Ron DeSantis, a figure who has captured the attention of the nation.

Through meticulous research and insightful analysis, we aim to reveal the man behind the public image, shedding light on the experiences and influences that have shaped his character and ideology.

Why is Ron DeSantis an important figure to write about? The answer lies in his rapid ascent to political prominence and the impact he has had on the state of Florida. As the 46th governor, DeSantis has been at the forefront of numerous policy initiatives, tackling critical issues ranging from the economy to education and public health. His leadership style, unwavering determination, and commitment to conservative principles have garnered both praise and criticism, making him a highly influential figure in American politics.

In the pages that follow, we will embark on a comprehensive journey through Ron DeSantis's life, from his childhood and education to his distinguished military career at the United States Naval Academy. We will explore his time at Yale Law School and his early legal career, setting the stage for his foray into politics.

This book will take an in-depth look at DeSantis's political career, starting with his early involvement and his campaigns for Congress. We will examine his legislative record and explore the major accomplishments of his first and second terms in Congress. The narrative will then shift to his bold decision to run for governor of Florida, detailing his campaign and the significant moments that led to his election victory.

As we delve into DeSantis's first year as governor, we will highlight his major accomplishments and initiatives, including his response to the COVID-19 pandemic. We will examine his economic policies, education reforms, and environmental initiatives, showcasing the breadth of his impact on the state of Florida.

Throughout this biography, we will explore the complex relationship between Ron DeSantis and former President Donald Trump, analyzing the impact of their alliance on DeSantis's political career and his standing within the Republican Party.

Moreover, we will not only focus on the public persona of Ron DeSantis but also seek to unveil the untold story behind the man. Through exclusive interviews, personal anecdotes, and behind-the-scenes accounts, we aim to offer readers an intimate glimpse into the lesser-known aspects of DeSantis's life and career, illuminating the experiences that have shaped his character and decision-making.

In summary, "The Biography of Ron DeSantis" provides a comprehensive account of the life and achievements of one of America's most influential political figures. By delving into his background, career, and personal journey, we aim to offer readers an engaging and informative exploration of the man who currently serves as the 46th governor of Florida. Join us as we embark on this captivating journey through the life of Ron DeSantis, uncovering the untold story of a remarkable leader.

Childhood and Education

In this chapter, we delve into the formative years of Ron DeSantis, exploring his childhood, family background, and educational journey. Through personal anecdotes and meticulous research, we aim to paint a vivid picture of the experiences that shaped the man who would go on to become the 46th governor of Florida.

Ron DeSantis was born on September 14, 1978, in the vibrant city of Jacksonville, Florida. Growing up in a middle-class family, he was raised with a strong sense of traditional values and a deep appreciation for the opportunities that America provided.

DeSantis's family background played a significant role in shaping his character and worldview. His parents, Karen and Ronald DeSantis Sr., instilled in him a sense of discipline, hard work, and dedication to service. His father, a hardworking construction worker, and his mother, a nurse, emphasized the importance of education and encouraged young Ron to pursue his dreams.

During his early years, DeSantis displayed an insatiable curiosity and a thirst for knowledge. From a young age, he excelled academically, demonstrating a sharp intellect and a natural talent for leadership. His teachers recognized his potential and often marveled at his ability to grasp complex concepts with ease.

DeSantis's educational journey began in kindergarten, where he quickly established himself as an attentive and diligent student. As he progressed through elementary school, his passion for learning grew, and he eagerly absorbed knowledge across various subjects. Mathematics, science, and history were among his favorites, and his teachers consistently praised his inquisitive nature and exceptional problem-solving skills.

During his middle school years, DeSantis continued to shine academically. He developed a reputation as a dedicated student, always going above and beyond in his pursuit of knowledge. However, his educational journey was not limited to the classroom alone. Outside of school, he actively engaged in extracurricular activities that fostered personal growth and honed his leadership skills.

One particular interest that captured DeSantis's attention during his childhood was sports. He displayed a natural athletic ability and participated in various sports teams, including baseball, basketball, and football. Through these experiences, he learned the value of teamwork, discipline, and perseverance, qualities that would later serve him well in his military and political endeavors.

In high school, DeSantis continued to excel academically while actively participating in student government and other leadership roles. His exceptional grades and leadership abilities garnered recognition from his peers and teachers, solidifying his reputation as a well-rounded student.

As he approached graduation, DeSantis faced a pivotal decision regarding his future. Drawing inspiration from his family's military background and his own deep sense of patriotism, he set his sights on attending the prestigious United States Naval Academy. The rigorous application process did not deter him, and through hard work and determination, he secured admission to the academy.

In conclusion, the early years of Ron DeSantis's life were characterized by a strong family foundation, a thirst for knowledge, and a drive to excel. From his supportive parents to his dedication to education and participation in extracurricular activities, these formative experiences laid the groundwork for his future achievements. Join us in the next chapter as we delve into DeSantis's remarkable journey at the United States Naval Academy and his subsequent military career, which would shape his path toward political leadership.

Naval Academy and Military Career

In this chapter, we delve into a transformative period in Ron DeSantis's life as we explore his decision to attend the United States Naval Academy, his rigorous training at the academy, and the remarkable military career that followed. Through personal accounts and meticulous research, we aim to provide readers with a vivid portrayal of DeSantis's experiences and achievements during this formative stage of his life.

Ron DeSantis's decision to attend the United States Naval Academy was a testament to his deep sense of duty, love for his country, and desire to serve in a meaningful capacity. Inspired by his family's military background, he recognized that the academy would provide him with a unique opportunity to receive a top-tier education while preparing him for a career in the military.

With unwavering determination, DeSantis embarked on a challenging journey at the Naval

Academy, embracing the demanding training and rigorous academic curriculum. The academy tested both his physical and mental fortitude, pushing him to his limits and shaping him into a disciplined and resilient leader.

During his time at the academy, DeSantis excelled academically, earning the respect and admiration of his peers and instructors. His dedication to his studies was matched by his commitment to his military training, where he demonstrated exceptional leadership skills and a deep understanding of military strategy and tactics.

The Naval Academy provided DeSantis with a multitude of opportunities to hone his leadership abilities and forge lifelong friendships with fellow cadets. Through team-oriented activities, he learned the value of collaboration, effective communication, and unwavering loyalty to his comrades—a testament to the camaraderie and ethos instilled in every cadet.

Upon graduation from the Naval Academy, DeSantis embarked on a remarkable military career that showcased his exemplary service and commitment to defending his country. He was commissioned as an officer in the United States Navy, where he quickly distinguished himself as a capable and dedicated leader.

Throughout his military career, DeSantis took on various roles and assignments that allowed him to showcase his leadership skills and contribute to the nation's defense. He served as a judge advocate, providing legal counsel and ensuring the proper administration of military justice. His dedication to upholding the principles of integrity and fairness earned him the respect of his peers and superiors.

DeSantis's military career also took him overseas, where he deployed to Iraq as part of Operation Iraqi Freedom. During his deployment, he demonstrated exceptional courage and leadership in the face of adversity, earning accolades for his unwavering commitment to his mission and the safety of his fellow servicemen and women.

In recognition of his service and accomplishments, DeSantis was awarded multiple military honors, including the Bronze Star Medal and the Iraq Campaign Medal. These accolades not only symbolize his bravery and dedication but also serve as a testament to his unwavering commitment to defending the values and principles of his country.

In conclusion, Ron DeSantis's time at the United States Naval Academy and his subsequent military career were defining periods that shaped his character, instilled discipline, and solidified his commitment to public service. The academy's rigorous training and the challenges he faced as a military officer prepared him for the leadership roles that lay ahead. Join us in the next chapter as we delve into DeSantis's journey through Yale Law School and his early legal career, which would serve as the stepping stones to his future political endeavors.

Yale Law School and Early Legal Career

In this chapter, we delve into an important phase of Ron DeSantis's life as we explore his decision to attend Yale Law School, his experiences during his time there, and the early stages of his legal career. Through personal insights and meticulous research, we aim to provide readers with a comprehensive understanding of DeSantis's journey through law school and his early contributions to the legal field.

The decision to attend Yale Law School marked a pivotal moment in Ron DeSantis's academic and professional trajectory. Recognized as one of the top law schools in the United States, Yale offered DeSantis an opportunity to further refine his legal acumen and expand his intellectual horizons. Driven by his passion for law and his desire to make a positive impact on society, he eagerly accepted the challenge.

DeSantis's time at Yale Law School was characterized by academic rigor, intellectual stimulation, and exposure to diverse perspectives. Immersed in a highly competitive and intellectually stimulating environment, he engaged in lively debates, honed his legal reasoning skills, and forged relationships with esteemed faculty and fellow students.

During his studies at Yale, DeSantis exhibited a thirst for knowledge and a keen interest in constitutional law and conservative legal principles. He distinguished himself as a diligent and exceptional student, earning recognition for his insightful contributions to classroom discussions and his ability to grasp complex legal concepts.

While at Yale, DeSantis's notable achievements extended beyond the classroom. He actively participated in various legal organizations, engaging in moot court competitions and serving in leadership roles that further enhanced his understanding of the law and provided valuable networking opportunities. These experiences helped shape his legal philosophy and solidify his commitment to upholding conservative principles.

Following his graduation from Yale Law School, DeSantis embarked on his early legal career. He began his professional journey as an attorney, where he dedicated his efforts to defending the rights and values he held dear. As a skilled litigator, he passionately advocated for his clients and demonstrated a deep understanding of the law.

Throughout his early legal career, DeSantis tackled a range of legal issues, working on cases that touched on constitutional matters, civil rights, and government regulations. His commitment to conservative principles guided his approach to legal practice, and he often sought to protect individual liberties and limited government intervention.

DeSantis's work as an attorney provided him with valuable insights into the legal system, and he became known for his meticulous research, persuasive arguments, and dedication to achieving justice. His commitment to upholding the rule of law and defending conservative values gained him the respect of colleagues and clients alike.

While practicing law, DeSantis also recognized the importance of public service and community engagement. He took an active role in local organizations and participated in pro bono work, demonstrating his commitment to giving back and making a positive impact on his community.

In conclusion, Ron DeSantis's decision to attend Yale Law School and his subsequent early legal career exemplified his intellectual curiosity, commitment to conservative principles, and dedication to the pursuit of justice. His time at law school and his work as an attorney laid the foundation for his future endeavors in politics, where he would continue to champion his beliefs and fight for the rights of the people. Join us in the next chapter as we explore DeSantis's entry into politics and his campaigns for Congress, which would mark the beginning of a new chapter in his remarkable journey.

Political Career Beginnings

In this chapter, we delve into the early political aspirations of Ron DeSantis, exploring his interest in politics, his initial involvement in the political arena, and his first campaign for Congress. Through personal anecdotes and comprehensive research, we aim to provide readers with a thorough understanding of DeSantis's early political career and the notable achievements that propelled him forward.

From an early age, Ron DeSantis demonstrated a keen interest in public service and a passion for making a difference in the lives of his fellow citizens. Inspired by the principles of limited government, individual liberty, and fiscal responsibility, he recognized the potential of politics as a platform to effect meaningful change.

DeSantis's initial involvement in politics can be traced back to his time as a student at Yale Law School. Recognizing the importance of engaging in the political process, he actively participated in conservative organizations and engaged in discussions on pressing political issues. These experiences not only deepened his understanding of policy but also sharpened his skills in articulating conservative values and principles.

Following his graduation from law school, DeSantis began to lay the foundation for his political career. He joined prestigious conservative think tanks, where he conducted in-depth research, authored influential policy papers, and contributed to the national conversation on critical issues. His work caught the attention of prominent conservative figures, who recognized his intellect, dedication, and commitment to advancing conservative ideals.

DeSantis's early political career saw him taking on various roles, each contributing to his growth as a leader and advocate for conservative principles. He served as a legal advisor to elected officials, where he provided invaluable insights on constitutional matters and played a key role in shaping policy initiatives.

Notably, DeSantis's first foray into electoral politics came with his campaign for Congress. In 2012, he decided to seek the Republican nomination for Florida's 6th congressional district. Armed with a deep understanding of policy issues, a fervent belief in limited government, and an unwavering commitment to serving his constituents, DeSantis embarked on a vigorous campaign to earn the support of the district's voters.

Throughout his campaign, DeSantis tirelessly crisscrossed the district, connecting with constituents, listening to their concerns, and sharing his vision for a more prosperous and limited government. His conservative platform, which emphasized fiscal responsibility, national security, and protecting individual liberties, resonated with many voters who sought a principled leader to represent their interests in Congress.

DeSantis's campaign was marked by his ability to effectively communicate his conservative values and his unwavering commitment to serving the people. He highlighted his military service, legal expertise, and dedication to the Constitution as key qualifications for the role he aspired to undertake.

With a compelling message and a strong grassroots organization, he successfully secured the Republican nomination, positioning himself as a formidable contender in the general election.

The general election proved to be a competitive battle, but DeSantis's tireless campaigning, charisma, and command of the issues propelled him to victory. In 2013, he was sworn in as a member of the United States House of Representatives, representing Florida's 6th congressional district.

In conclusion, Ron DeSantis's early political career was characterized by his deep-rooted conservative values, dedication to public service, and an unwavering commitment to making a positive impact on his community. From his involvement in conservative organizations to his successful campaign for Congress, he showcased his ability to articulate conservative principles and connect with voters. Join us in the next chapter as we explore DeSantis's tenure in Congress and the notable achievements that marked this phase of his political journey.

First Term in Congress

In this chapter, we delve into Ron DeSantis's election to Congress and his first term in office. We explore his legislative record, notable accomplishments, and the impact he made during this crucial period of his political career. Through personal anecdotes and extensive research, we aim to provide readers with a comprehensive understanding of DeSantis's early tenure as a member of the United States House of Representatives.

Ron DeSantis's election to Congress marked a significant milestone in his political journey. With a strong commitment to conservative principles and a compelling vision for limited government, he captured the attention and support of voters in Florida's 6th congressional district. In 2013, he was sworn in as their representative, carrying the hopes and aspirations of his constituents to the hallowed halls of Congress.

During his first term in office, DeSantis wasted no time in making his mark as a principled and effective legislator. Drawing on his legal background, his military experience, and a deep understanding of conservative values, he championed legislation that reflected his commitment to fiscal responsibility, limited government intervention, and the protection of individual liberties.

DeSantis's legislative record during his first term was characterized by his unwavering dedication to conservative principles. He co-sponsored bills aimed at reducing the size and scope of the federal government, advocating for balanced budgets, and fostering economic growth through pro-growth policies. His emphasis on reducing regulations and empowering individuals and businesses resonated with many constituents who sought a government that respected their rights and freedoms.

Furthermore, DeSantis played an active role in shaping legislation related to national security and foreign policy. Drawing on his military background, he provided valuable insights and expertise, working to strengthen America's defense capabilities and ensure the safety and security of the nation and its citizens.

Notable accomplishments marked DeSantis's first term in Congress. He worked tirelessly to repeal burdensome regulations that stifled economic growth and hindered job creation. His efforts resulted in the passage of legislation that eliminated unnecessary red tape, providing relief to small businesses and fostering an environment conducive to innovation and entrepreneurship.

Moreover, DeSantis played a pivotal role in advancing legislation that aimed to strengthen national security and protect American interests abroad. His expertise in foreign policy and national defense allowed him to provide thoughtful contributions to discussions on these critical issues, earning him respect from colleagues on both sides of the aisle.

In recognition of his exceptional legislative record and his commitment to conservative principles, DeSantis garnered widespread support and admiration. His unwavering dedication to his constituents and his ability to effectively advocate for their needs and concerns earned him a reputation as a principled and results-oriented representative.

In conclusion, Ron DeSantis's first term in Congress exemplified his commitment to conservative values, his dedication to public service, and his ability to effect change through principled leadership. Throughout this crucial period, he demonstrated his legislative acumen, advocating for limited government, fiscal responsibility, and a robust national defense. Join us in the next chapter as we explore DeSantis's re-election campaign and his continued service as a congressman, laying the groundwork for his future political aspirations.

Second Term in Congress

In this chapter, we delve into Ron DeSantis's reelection to Congress and his second term in office. We explore his legislative record, notable accomplishments, and the impact he made during this important phase of his political career. Through personal anecdotes and extensive research, we aim to provide readers with a comprehensive understanding of DeSantis's continued service as a member of the United States House of Representatives.

Ron DeSantis's successful reelection to Congress affirmed the trust and support of his constituents in Florida's 6th congressional district. Bolstered by his accomplishments and unwavering commitment to conservative principles, he embarked on his second term with renewed vigor and determination to make a positive impact on behalf of the people he represented.

During his second term in office, DeSantis built upon his legislative record and pursued policies that aligned with his conservative values. Drawing on his experiences and insights gained during his first term, he continued to champion fiscal responsibility, limited government intervention, and the protection of individual liberties.

DeSantis's legislative record during his second term showcased his tenacity and ability to effect change. He actively sponsored and supported bills aimed at reducing government waste, cutting unnecessary spending, and promoting economic growth. His emphasis on responsible governance resonated with constituents who sought a government that prioritized fiscal discipline and acted as a steward of taxpayer resources.

Furthermore, DeSantis remained deeply engaged in matters of national security and foreign policy. Leveraging his military background and expertise, he contributed to the development of legislation that bolstered America's defense capabilities, safeguarded the nation against emerging threats, and promoted a strong and secure homeland.

Notable accomplishments marked DeSantis's second term in Congress. He spearheaded efforts to enact tax reforms that provided relief to hardworking Americans, spurring economic growth and job creation. His advocacy for lower tax rates and a simplified tax code reflected his commitment to empowering individuals and fostering an environment conducive to prosperity.

Moreover, DeSantis played a pivotal role in advancing legislation aimed at promoting transparency and accountability in government. He pushed for greater oversight and stricter adherence to constitutional principles, working to restore public trust in the institutions of democracy.

Throughout his second term, DeSantis continued to prioritize constituent service, ensuring that the needs and concerns of the people he represented were heard and addressed. He remained accessible and engaged, regularly holding town hall meetings and listening to the perspectives of his constituents. This commitment to effective representation earned him the respect and admiration of those he served.

In recognition of his outstanding legislative record, principled leadership, and commitment to his constituents, DeSantis solidified his position as a prominent figure in conservative politics. His ability to navigate the complexities of Capitol Hill, build coalitions, and advance meaningful legislation set him apart as a formidable legislator.

In conclusion, Ron DeSantis's second term in Congress demonstrated his continued dedication to conservative principles, his effectiveness as a legislator, and his commitment to serving the people he represented. Throughout this crucial period, he contributed to policy debates, advanced conservative values, and worked tirelessly to promote the best interests of his constituents. Join us in the next chapter as we explore DeSantis's decision to embark on a new chapter in his political career, seeking higher office and aiming to make an even greater impact on the state of Florida.

Run for Governor of Florida

In this chapter, we explore Ron DeSantis's decision to run for the governorship of Florida, his gubernatorial campaign, and the notable moments and achievements that shaped his path to victory. Through personal anecdotes and extensive research, we aim to provide readers with a comprehensive understanding of DeSantis's journey from congressman to gubernatorial candidate.

Ron DeSantis's decision to run for the governorship of Florida was driven by his deep commitment to public service and his vision for a better future for the state. Inspired by his experiences in Congress and fueled by a desire to enact conservative policies at the state level, DeSantis saw the opportunity to make a significant impact by leading Florida as its governor.

The decision to embark on a gubernatorial campaign was not taken lightly. DeSantis recognized the magnitude of the undertaking and the responsibility that would come with leading one of the most populous and diverse states in the nation. He believed that his conservative principles, combined with his record of effective leadership and his dedication to the people of Florida, uniquely positioned him to address the pressing challenges facing the state.

DeSantis's gubernatorial campaign was marked by a tireless commitment to connect with voters and articulate his vision for Florida's future. Drawing on his experiences as a congressman, he emphasized his track record of conservative accomplishments and his commitment to limited government, economic growth, and individual liberties.

Throughout the campaign, DeSantis crisscrossed the state, engaging with constituents from all walks of life, listening to their concerns, and sharing his vision for a stronger and more prosperous Florida. He held town halls, participated in debates, and attended numerous community events, allowing voters to get to know him personally and understand his policy positions.

Notable moments and achievements punctuated DeSantis's gubernatorial campaign, capturing the attention and support of voters across the state. His endorsement by influential conservative figures, including President Donald J. Trump, bolstered his campaign and solidified his standing within the Republican Party.

Moreover, DeSantis distinguished himself through his clear and concise messaging, focusing on key issues such as job creation, education reform, public safety, and protecting Florida's natural resources. His ability to connect with voters on a personal level, coupled with his policy expertise, resonated with many Floridians who sought a leader with a proven track record and a compelling vision for the state's future.

The victory in the gubernatorial election was a culmination of DeSantis's relentless dedication and the unwavering support of his campaign team and grassroots supporters. His commitment to conservative values, his ability to effectively communicate his message, and his deep understanding of the issues facing Floridians propelled him to victory, as voters entrusted him with the responsibility of leading the state.

Ron DeSantis's election as the governor of Florida marked a significant milestone in his political career. It symbolized the culmination of years of public service, principled leadership, and a steadfast commitment to making a positive impact on the lives of his fellow citizens. As he prepared to assume the role of Florida's chief executive, he knew that the challenges ahead would be significant, but he was ready to face them head-on.

In conclusion, Ron DeSantis's decision to run for governor of Florida, his gubernatorial campaign, and his victory in the election demonstrated his unwavering dedication to public service, his ability to connect with voters, and his commitment to advancing conservative principles. Join us in the next chapter as we explore the early days of DeSantis's tenure as the governor of Florida and the transformative policies and achievements that defined his leadership.

First Year as Governor

In this chapter, we delve into Ron DeSantis's first year as the governor of Florida, examining the major accomplishments, initiatives, challenges, and controversies that shaped his early tenure. Through personal anecdotes and comprehensive research, we aim to provide readers with a vivid and insightful account of DeSantis's transformative leadership during this pivotal period.

Ron DeSantis's first year as governor marked the beginning of a new chapter in his political career. Guided by his conservative principles and fueled by a passion for public service, he wasted no time in taking action to fulfill his campaign promises and advance his vision for the state of Florida.

From the outset, DeSantis demonstrated a proactive and results-driven approach to governance. He swiftly assembled a talented team of advisers and cabinet members, each dedicated to translating his vision into tangible policy initiatives. This collaborative effort laid the foundation for a productive and impactful first year in office.

One of DeSantis's major accomplishments during his first year as governor was his unwavering commitment to education reform. Recognizing the vital role education plays in shaping the future of Florida, he championed initiatives to increase school choice options, expand career and technical education, and elevate the quality of education across the state. By prioritizing the needs of students and empowering parents, DeSantis sought to create an educational system that fostered innovation, excellence, and opportunity.

Furthermore, DeSantis made significant strides in revitalizing Florida's economy. His administration implemented policies aimed at attracting businesses, creating jobs, and stimulating economic growth. Through targeted tax reforms, deregulation efforts, and strategic investments in infrastructure, DeSantis fostered an environment conducive to entrepreneurship and prosperity. His focus on promoting a business-friendly climate positioned Florida as a national leader in job creation and economic expansion.

In the realm of public safety, DeSantis took decisive action to address pressing concerns and ensure the well-being of Floridians. He prioritized the protection of communities by enacting legislation that strengthened penalties for violent crimes, supported law enforcement agencies, and improved public safety infrastructure. By championing policies that prioritize the safety and security of all Floridians, DeSantis demonstrated his commitment to fostering a state where families and individuals could thrive.

However, DeSantis's first year as governor was not without challenges and controversies. Like any leader, he faced criticism and opposition from various quarters. Some of the notable controversies during this period included debates over environmental policies, healthcare reforms, and immigration enforcement. These challenges tested DeSantis's ability to navigate complex issues and find common ground while staying true to his conservative principles and the best interests of the state.

Despite the challenges, DeSantis remained steadfast in his commitment to delivering results for the people of Florida. His ability to communicate his policies effectively, engage with diverse stakeholders, and remain focused on the needs of the state allowed him to overcome obstacles and drive meaningful change.

In conclusion, Ron DeSantis's first year as governor of Florida showcased his transformative leadership, unwavering commitment to conservative principles, and his ability to deliver results. Through education reform, economic revitalization, and prioritizing public safety, DeSantis demonstrated his dedication to building a stronger and more prosperous Florida. Join us in the next chapter as we explore the subsequent years of DeSantis's tenure, highlighting the significant accomplishments and challenges he encountered during this period of his governorship.

Response to COVID-19 Pandemic

In this chapter, we delve into Ron DeSantis's response to the COVID-19 pandemic in Florida, examining his approach, notable decisions, and the criticisms and praise he received during this challenging period. Through personal narratives and extensive research, we aim to provide readers with a comprehensive understanding of DeSantis's leadership during one of the most significant public health crises of our time.

The COVID-19 pandemic presented unprecedented challenges to leaders across the globe, and Ron DeSantis, as the governor of Florida, faced the immense responsibility of safeguarding the health and well-being of millions of Floridians. As the virus spread and cases surged, DeSantis quickly took action to mitigate the impact and protect the state's residents.

DeSantis's response to the pandemic in Florida was multifaceted, combining public health measures, economic considerations, and a focus on individual liberties. One of the key aspects of his approach was to balance the need to protect public health with minimizing the economic impact on businesses and individuals. He implemented measures to safeguard vulnerable populations, ramp up testing and contact tracing efforts, and provide resources to healthcare providers.

Throughout the pandemic, DeSantis made notable decisions that shaped the course of Florida's response. One of the early decisions was the establishment of a comprehensive testing program to identify and track the spread of the virus. By expanding testing capabilities, DeSantis aimed to provide timely information to guide targeted interventions and protect vulnerable populations.

Another significant decision was the implementation of guidelines for reopening businesses and the economy. DeSantis recognized the importance of supporting economic activity while ensuring the safety of the public. He took steps to reopen businesses in a phased approach, considering regional variations and data-driven indicators to guide the process.

DeSantis also prioritized the vaccination efforts in Florida, working to ensure efficient distribution and administration of vaccines. He established vaccination sites, expanded eligibility criteria, and collaborated with federal and local partners to expedite the vaccination rollout. His goal was to protect as many Floridians as possible, particularly the elderly and those at higher risk of severe illness.

As with any crisis, DeSantis's response to the pandemic faced both criticisms and praise. Critics argued that he did not take sufficient early action to curb the spread of the virus, while others questioned the timing and pace of reopening measures. Some disagreed with his approach to mask mandates and other mitigation strategies, citing concerns about public health. These criticisms highlighted the complexities and differing perspectives surrounding pandemic response.

However, DeSantis also garnered praise for his efforts. Supporters commended his focus on individual liberties and personal responsibility, advocating for a balanced approach that considered the economic and mental health consequences of lockdown measures. They applauded his commitment to reopening schools, recognizing the importance of in-person education for students' well-being and development.

In navigating the challenges of the pandemic, DeSantis faced an immense task of making difficult decisions with limited information and conflicting advice. His response to the COVID-19 pandemic reflected a delicate balancing act between protecting public health and addressing the broader impacts on society.

In conclusion, Ron DeSantis's response to the COVID-19 pandemic in Florida was marked by a commitment to safeguarding public health while considering the economic and individual implications. By implementing testing programs, guiding reopening efforts, and prioritizing vaccinations, he aimed to strike a balance between protecting lives and livelihoods. The criticisms and praise he received underscore the complexity of pandemic response and the diverse perspectives surrounding it. Join us in the next chapter as we explore the subsequent chapters of DeSantis's governorship, highlighting his ongoing initiatives and the impact of his leadership on the state of Florida.

Economic Policies and Job Growth

In this chapter, we explore Ron DeSantis's economic policies and his efforts to stimulate job growth and improve the economy in Florida. Through personal anecdotes and thorough research, we aim to provide readers with a comprehensive understanding of his approach, notable achievements, and the challenges he faced in this crucial area of governance.

As governor of Florida, Ron DeSantis prioritized economic prosperity and job creation. Recognizing the vital role a thriving economy plays in the well-being of Floridians, he implemented a series of policies and initiatives aimed at attracting businesses, fostering entrepreneurship, and stimulating economic growth.

DeSantis's economic policies were anchored in principles of fiscal responsibility, limited government intervention, and free-market principles. He believed in creating an environment that incentivized businesses to invest, innovate, and flourish, ultimately leading to job creation and economic expansion.

One of the key pillars of DeSantis's economic agenda was tax reform. He championed measures to reduce taxes, making Florida more competitive and attractive to businesses. By lowering the tax burden on individuals and corporations, DeSantis aimed to stimulate economic activity, attract investments, and create a favorable climate for job growth.

In addition to tax reform, DeSantis focused on cutting unnecessary regulations that hindered business growth and stifled innovation. He streamlined bureaucratic processes and eliminated red tape, making it easier for entrepreneurs to start and expand their businesses. By fostering a business-friendly environment, DeSantis sought to unleash the entrepreneurial spirit and drive economic prosperity across the state.

DeSantis also recognized the importance of strategic investments in infrastructure to support economic growth. He championed initiatives to improve transportation networks, enhance broadband connectivity, and invest in critical infrastructure projects. These efforts aimed to facilitate commerce, attract new industries, and create job opportunities in various sectors.

Under DeSantis's leadership, Florida experienced significant job growth and economic expansion. His focus on creating an environment conducive to business growth led to the addition of thousands of new jobs in sectors such as technology, manufacturing, tourism, and healthcare. Unemployment rates dropped, and Floridians had increased access to quality employment opportunities.

Notable achievements during DeSantis's tenure include the successful attraction of major companies to the state, resulting in significant job creation and economic investment. His administration worked tirelessly to incentivize companies to relocate or expand their operations in Florida, highlighting the state's competitive advantages, such as its low-tax environment, skilled workforce, and quality of life.

However, DeSantis also faced challenges in his pursuit of economic growth. The COVID-19 pandemic presented unforeseen obstacles, disrupting industries and causing economic uncertainty. DeSantis had to adapt his strategies to navigate the unprecedented circumstances, implementing measures to support struggling businesses, provide financial relief, and position the state for a strong recovery.

In conclusion, Ron DeSantis's economic policies and commitment to job growth played a vital role in Florida's economic success during his tenure as governor. Through tax reform, regulatory relief, and strategic investments, he fostered an environment that attracted businesses, created jobs, and propelled economic expansion. The challenges posed by the pandemic further tested his leadership, but his adaptive approach demonstrated resilience and determination to support Florida's economic recovery. Join us in the next chapter as we delve into other significant aspects of DeSantis's governorship, highlighting his legislative agenda, social policies, and impact on the state's communities.

Education Policy and School Choice

In this chapter, we delve into Ron DeSantis's education policy as governor of Florida, examining his efforts to promote school choice and improve the education system in the state. Through personal narratives and extensive research, we aim to provide readers with a comprehensive understanding of his approach, notable achievements, and the challenges he encountered in this critical area of governance.

Education has always been a priority for Ron DeSantis, recognizing its pivotal role in shaping the future of Florida's children and the state's overall prosperity. As governor, he sought to implement policies that would empower parents, expand educational opportunities, and elevate the quality of education for all students.

DeSantis was a strong advocate for school choice, believing that parents should have the freedom to choose the educational pathway that best suits their children's needs. He championed policies that expanded school choice options, including charter schools, private schools, and scholarship programs. By providing alternatives to traditional public schools, DeSantis aimed to create a competitive and innovative educational landscape.

One of the key initiatives in DeSantis's education policy was the expansion of voucher programs and scholarship opportunities. He worked to increase the availability of private school scholarships, empowering low-income families to access quality education that was previously beyond their reach. Through these programs, DeSantis aimed to level the playing field and ensure that every child, regardless of their socioeconomic background, had the opportunity to receive a high-quality education.

DeSantis also recognized the importance of early childhood education in setting a strong foundation for children's academic success. He prioritized investments in early childhood programs, such as pre-kindergarten education, to ensure that children entered school prepared and ready to learn. By expanding access to quality early education,

DeSantis aimed to narrow achievement gaps and foster long-term educational attainment.

In his pursuit of education improvement, DeSantis focused on elevating the teaching profession and empowering educators. He advocated for increased teacher salaries, recognizing the vital role teachers play in students' lives and the importance of attracting and retaining talented educators. DeSantis also supported initiatives to provide professional development opportunities and resources to enhance teaching effectiveness.

Under DeSantis's leadership, Florida witnessed notable achievements in education. The expansion of school choice options provided parents with greater control over their children's education, allowing them to select schools that aligned with their values, priorities, and educational goals. The scholarship programs opened doors of opportunity for disadvantaged students, offering them a chance at a high-quality education that could transform their lives.

However, DeSantis's education policies were not without challenges. Critics voiced concerns about the potential diversion of resources from public schools and questioned the impact of increased school choice on traditional public education. There were also debates surrounding the accountability and oversight of private schools participating in voucher programs.

DeSantis navigated these challenges by emphasizing the importance of accountability and transparency in education. He sought to implement measures to ensure that all schools, regardless of their governance structure, met high standards of quality and performance. By holding schools accountable for student outcomes and requiring transparency in reporting, DeSantis aimed to provide parents with the information they needed to make informed choices about their children's education.

In conclusion, Ron DeSantis's education policy as governor of Florida reflected his commitment to empowering parents, expanding school choice, and improving educational opportunities for all students. Through the promotion of school choice, expansion of scholarship programs, and investments in early childhood education, DeSantis aimed to create a robust educational ecosystem that catered to the diverse needs of Florida's students. While challenges existed, his focus on accountability and transparency demonstrated a dedication to ensuring quality education for all. Join us in the next chapter as we explore other significant aspects of DeSantis's governorship.

Environmental Policies and Conservation Efforts

In this chapter, we delve into Ron DeSantis's environmental policies as governor of Florida, exploring his efforts to protect and conserve the state's natural resources. Through personal narratives and extensive research, we aim to provide readers with a comprehensive understanding of his approach, notable achievements, and the challenges he encountered in this crucial area of governance.

Florida's unique natural beauty and diverse ecosystems have always held a special place in Ron DeSantis's heart. Recognizing the importance of preserving these resources for future generations, he made environmental conservation a priority during his tenure as governor.

DeSantis's environmental policies were centered around sustainable development, conservation, and addressing the challenges posed by climate change. He understood that striking a balance between economic growth and environmental protection was essential for the long-term well-being of Florida's communities and natural heritage.

One of the key aspects of DeSantis's environmental agenda was the restoration and protection of Florida's water bodies. He launched initiatives to address water quality issues, such as harmful algal blooms and pollution in the state's rivers, lakes, and coastal areas. Through increased funding, improved infrastructure, and partnerships with stakeholders, DeSantis aimed to ensure clean and healthy water resources for both ecological health and human consumption.

DeSantis also prioritized the conservation of Florida's unique ecosystems, such as the Everglades and the Florida Keys. He recognized the significance of these areas for biodiversity, tourism, and the overall ecological balance of the state. Under his leadership, efforts were made to restore and preserve these fragile ecosystems, including investments in habitat restoration, invasive species management, and increased protection measures.

In his commitment to addressing climate change, DeSantis took steps to mitigate its impacts and prepare Florida for a more resilient future. He established the Office of Resilience and Coastal Protection to coordinate state-wide efforts in adapting to rising sea levels and extreme weather events. DeSantis also prioritized renewable energy development, supporting initiatives to increase solar energy production and reduce greenhouse gas emissions.

During his tenure, DeSantis achieved notable accomplishments in the realm of environmental conservation. He signed legislation to combat harmful algal blooms and improve water quality, demonstrating his dedication to protecting Florida's delicate aquatic ecosystems. The Everglades restoration efforts received renewed attention and funding under his administration, with a focus on reducing nutrient pollution and restoring natural water flow.

However, DeSantis's environmental policies were not without challenges and controversies. Some critics raised concerns about the balance between economic development and environmental protection, while others advocated for more aggressive measures to address climate change. The delicate balance between the needs of industry and the preservation of natural resources required careful navigation, and DeSantis faced both support and opposition in his environmental initiatives.

In conclusion, Ron DeSantis's environmental policies as governor of Florida demonstrated his commitment to preserving the state's natural resources, addressing water quality issues, and taking steps towards climate resilience. Through sustainable development, conservation efforts, and investments in renewable energy, he aimed to create a harmonious balance between economic growth and environmental protection. Join us in the next chapter as we explore other significant aspects of DeSantis's governorship and the impact he had on the lives of Floridians.

Relationship with Donald Trump

In this chapter, we delve into the relationship between Ron DeSantis and former President Donald Trump, examining their political alliance, notable moments, controversies, and the impact of their association on DeSantis's political career. Through personal narratives and extensive research, we aim to provide readers with a comprehensive understanding of the dynamics between these two influential figures and the implications for DeSantis's trajectory as a politician.

Ron DeSantis's rise to political prominence coincided with the presidency of Donald Trump. Their relationship began during DeSantis's campaign for governor of Florida in 2018 when he received an endorsement from then-President Trump. This endorsement proved pivotal to DeSantis's victory, as Trump's support resonated with a significant portion of Florida's Republican base.

The endorsement was followed by a series of joint campaign appearances and rallies where DeSantis and Trump showcased their alignment on key issues such as immigration, conservative values, and economic policies. Their shared vision and messaging strengthened their bond and solidified DeSantis's reputation as a candidate aligned with Trump's agenda.

Throughout his tenure as governor, DeSantis maintained a close relationship with the former president. They exchanged ideas, consulted on policy matters, and occasionally made joint public appearances. Their alignment on issues such as immigration reform, tax cuts, and conservative judicial appointments further solidified their political alliance.

Notably, DeSantis's association with Trump was not without controversy. Some critics accused DeSantis of being too closely aligned with the former president and argued that he prioritized loyalty to Trump over the interests of Florida's diverse population. However, DeSantis defended his relationship with Trump, highlighting the benefits of having a strong rapport with the sitting president and leveraging it to deliver results for the state.

One of the most significant moments in their relationship came during the COVID-19 pandemic. DeSantis closely aligned his approach to handling the crisis with Trump's policies and messaging. This included resisting statewide lockdowns, emphasizing the importance of reopening the economy, and downplaying the severity of the virus at times. While these actions garnered criticism from some quarters, they also resonated with Trump's base of supporters.

The association with Trump has undoubtedly played a significant role in shaping DeSantis's political career. It has provided him with a national platform and elevated his profile among conservative voters. The endorsement and support from Trump propelled DeSantis's gubernatorial campaign and helped solidify his position as a rising star within the Republican Party.

Moreover, the relationship with Trump has also impacted DeSantis's policy decisions and governing style. He has adopted a populist approach, appealing to Trump's base and positioning himself as a champion of conservative values. This alignment has garnered support from Trump loyalists and positioned DeSantis as a potential contender for higher office in the future.

However, as with any political alliance, there are potential risks and challenges. The controversies and polarizing nature of Trump's presidency may present hurdles for DeSantis in appealing to a broader electorate beyond the conservative base. Striking a balance between maintaining his own identity and navigating the influence of Trump's legacy will be a delicate task for DeSantis as he seeks to expand his political reach.

In conclusion, Ron DeSantis's relationship with former President Donald Trump has had a profound impact on his political career. The endorsement, shared policy goals, and joint appearances with Trump bolstered DeSantis's candidacy and contributed to his victory in the gubernatorial race. While their alliance has faced criticisms and controversies, it has also provided DeSantis with a national platform and solidified his standing among conservative voters. The implications of this relationship on DeSantis's future ambitions and his ability to appeal to a broader electorate.

Future Political Aspirations

In this chapter, we explore Ron DeSantis's potential future political aspirations, analyze his chances of success in any future campaigns or endeavors, and discuss what the future may hold for his political career. Drawing from his past achievements, public perception, and the current political landscape, we aim to provide readers with insights into DeSantis's ambitions and prospects moving forward.

Throughout his career, Ron DeSantis has demonstrated a drive for public service and a passion for making a difference in the lives of Floridians. His successful tenure as governor of Florida has positioned him as a rising star within the Republican Party and has sparked speculation about his potential future political ambitions.

One of the most widely discussed possibilities for DeSantis is a run for the presidency of the United States. His alignment with former President Donald Trump, coupled with his conservative policies and strong support among Republican voters, has fueled speculation about his presidential aspirations. DeSantis's popularity within the party and his ability to resonate with conservative voters make him a potentially formidable candidate in future Republican primary contests.

However, the path to the presidency is fraught with challenges and competition. DeSantis would likely face a crowded field of Republican contenders, each vying for the nomination. While his association with Trump may play to his advantage with the conservative base, he would also need to navigate the broader electorate and appeal to a diverse range of voters.

Another potential avenue for DeSantis is seeking reelection as governor of Florida. If he decides to run for a second term, his strong incumbency advantage and popularity among Republican voters could position him as the front-runner in the race. The success of his first term, marked by conservative policy accomplishments, economic growth, and a vocal response to the COVID-19 pandemic, has solidified his standing among supporters and may provide a strong foundation for a reelection campaign.

Beyond the presidency or gubernatorial reelection, DeSantis may also explore other political avenues, such as a run for the U.S. Senate or a position within a Republican administration. His background as a military veteran, his legal expertise, and his legislative experience in Congress make him a viable candidate for high-level appointments or leadership roles within the party.

While DeSantis's potential future political aspirations generate excitement and speculation, it is important to recognize that the political landscape is ever-changing. Factors such as shifting public opinion, unforeseen events, and the emergence of new leaders can greatly influence the trajectory of a politician's career.

It is also worth noting that political aspirations are not solely determined by personal ambition, but also by the support and encouragement of a politician's base and political allies. The receptiveness of the Republican Party, its voter base, and influential figures within the party will play a crucial role in shaping DeSantis's future political path.

In assessing DeSantis's chances of success in any future campaigns or endeavors, several factors must be considered. His ability to maintain and expand his support base, effectively communicate his policies and achievements, navigate potential controversies, and adapt to the evolving political landscape will all play pivotal roles in determining his prospects.

Furthermore, the outcome of the 2022 and 2024 elections, as well as the broader political climate, will have implications for DeSantis's political trajectory. The performance of the Republican Party and the public's perception of his governance in Florida will shape the narrative surrounding his potential candidacy.

In conclusion, Ron DeSantis's future political aspirations are subject to speculation and uncertainty. His successful tenure as governor of Florida and his alignment with former President Donald Trump have positioned him as a rising star within the Republican Party. The presidency, gubernatorial reelection, a senatorial run, or a high-level appointment are all potential avenues for Ron DeSantis to explore in the future. As with any political career, success will depend on various factors, including the evolving political landscape, public sentiment, and the support of key stakeholders.

Conclusion

As we conclude the captivating journey through the life and career of Ron DeSantis, we find ourselves in awe of the remarkable accomplishments, unwavering dedication, and steadfast commitment that have defined his path. From his humble beginnings to his current position as the governor of Florida, DeSantis has demonstrated resilience, vision, and a genuine passion for public service. This biography has provided an intimate glimpse into the personal and political aspects of his life, allowing readers to understand the man behind the public figure.

But this is not the end of the story. Ron DeSantis's journey is far from over, and the future holds countless possibilities for him. As we have explored in the previous chapter, DeSantis has potential future political aspirations that could propel him to even greater heights. Will he seek higher office? Will he continue to champion the causes he holds dear? Only time will reveal the answers to these questions.

In the coming years, we can expect to witness the continued growth and evolution of Ron DeSantis as a political leader. His strategic thinking, unwavering commitment to conservative values, and ability to connect with the people of Florida have already earned him a prominent place in the national political landscape. With his rising popularity and strong track record, he has become a formidable force in American politics.

As readers, we are left with a sense of anticipation, eagerly awaiting the next chapters of Ron DeSantis's story. What new accomplishments will he achieve? What challenges will he face? How will he continue to shape the political landscape of Florida and beyond? These questions linger in our minds, driving our curiosity and keeping us engaged in the ongoing narrative of his life and career.

On behalf of the readers, we extend our best wishes to Ron DeSantis on his future political aspirations. May he continue to lead with integrity, conviction, and a steadfast dedication to the people he serves. The journey may have brought us to the end of this biography, but it marks only the beginning of an exciting and promising future for Ron DeSantis.

To stay informed and to ensure you don't miss any future books in the "Real Facts" series, be sure to keep an eye out for the next installment, where we delve into the untold stories and fascinating insights of another influential figure. By exploring the lives of remarkable individuals like Ron DeSantis, we gain a deeper understanding of the political landscape and the individuals shaping our world.

Thank you for joining us on this compelling journey through the biography of Ron DeSantis. We hope this book has provided you with a comprehensive, informative, and engaging exploration of his life, accomplishments, and the untold stories that have shaped him. Remember to visit "Real Facts" on Amazon for more enlightening biographies that delve into the lives of prominent figures and shed light on their impactful contributions.

In the words of Ron DeSantis himself, "*We're just getting started*."

Made in the USA
Columbia, SC
25 May 2023

17276555R00039